The Making of a Holy Man

Kathy Little Wolf

Front Porch History
2013

Copyright © 2012, 2013 Kathy Little Wolf. All rights reserved.
ISBN: 978-0-9855969-6-5

Dedication

This book is dedicated to the Creator God, whom I love with all my heart, mind, body, and soul. It is the Creator that lead Rudy to guide me, to teach me, and to tell me this book was to be written. I thank You, Creator, for the countless blessings You have bestowed on me, and the brother You graced me with on this glorious journey.

I write this book out of love for my dear friend and brother. I love and adore you. I am grateful to you for following the Red Road in the manner The Creator God has led you to do. May the Creator, The Great Mystery, guide you, protect you, shower you with His grace and mercy, and bless you with all the love you can stand.

Much love and respect to you, Rudy.

Kathy

What I have learned from the Creator God is: the greatest of all medicine is love . . . along with honesty and truth. It is one family, one circle, one love, one pipe . . . and one Creator; and I encourage all to put the Creator God first above all things in life. To love one another with the greatest love . . . and take care of each as one would their own self and own spirit in a sacred manner . . .

Rudy Escamilla

The Making of a Holy Man

When I arrived in South Dakota I knew my life was about to change, but I had no idea how much. I went there with the intention of learning healing of the mind, body and spirit . . . I received this, and so much more.

It all started on Facebook. Go figure, right? I've seen my share of so-called medicine men on many social sites and have found very few to be real. When a good friend told me about Rudy, I held my tongue, rolled my eyes, and thought, "Here we go again." I watched him from a distance for a time, and I have to admit my interest grew. He didn't call himself a medicine man, and when I dug a little deeper I saw why he referred to himself as a "Holy Man," and it only got more interesting from there.

I was more than a little surprised to see he professed openly he was also a Christian. By this time I was more curious than ever. I did what anyone would do and sent the friend request and continued watching. This was a new one for me . . . I had to know more. I have seen others try to attack him, attack his faith, attack his "Indianness," if you will . . . he never wavered. He stood his ground, he stood strong, but he did not stand alone. Never asking for anyone's approval, not asking for followers, and never once asking for money . . . or anything else. Something that started out as almost entertainment for me (simply because I went in expecting the worst and to be disappointed again since so many play the game in the name of God and all to make a profit) turned into a great friendship and a deep respect for this man. We began to talk on the phone, and the more we talked, the more I learned. I learned about him, his family, and the Lakota people. He even managed to teach me about myself (I certainly did not expect that), and most importantly, I learned about the Creator God. I figured out pretty quickly I didn't know as much as I thought, and it seems maybe I wasn't the only one playing the "sit back and watch" game.

One day he asked me to help out with an "event page" for him online, and I agreed. Little did I know my life was beginning to change, in a big way. The event was Sundance to be held in Rudy's hometown in South Dakota. I put all the information he asked me to on the page, including dates, time, what to bring, what not to bring. There are "rules," if you will, and all must abide by them or they will be asked to leave.

I toyed with the idea of going for months, it seemed . . . then I prayed about it. (Don't pray unless you expect answers, and the answer may not be what you expect or want to hear.) I went from toying with the idea to not being able to think of anything else. Then I got a call . . . it was Rudy.

We chatted for awhile and we had a good talk, then he laid it on me. "You will be there," he said. I just laughed and said, "Oh . . . okay, how do you know?" Through Rudy, the Creator had me right where he wanted me, and Rudy responded, "Creator said you would be." There was no hesitation in his words or humor in his voice; it was just very matter of fact. My head was spinning. I'd gone from thinking "I can't go, I can't afford this trip," to thinking "I have to go, I can't afford not to."

The friend who had introduced us online, Rose Butler, called me a day or two later and, of course, she was worked up over this. She and her family were going. I could literally feel the excitement in her voice. I just listened while in the back of my mind I kept hearing Rudy's words rotate through my brain. Rose said, "Call the bus station and find out how much it is for you to get there. I'm going to pay your way." BAM! There it is . . . they were teaming up on me.

Who are these people, I wondered? Rudy and Rose were working for "Team God" and I must say, as for the Creator . . . never doubt the Creator's sense of humor. As for me, I was out of excuses. If I really wanted my spirituality to go to the next level it was time to make the move forward or be content with constantly wondering "what if" for the rest of my life.

I waited a long time before discussing it with my husband simply because I didn't really think I was going. The dreaded conversation began and I was stunned. He not only agreed with but supported my going to this event. He took it a step further and bought me tickets to fly out and arrive the day before it all began. The deal was done. I couldn't back out now if I wanted to.

When my husband called me the next day and said, "Honey, I got your plane tickets today. I'll bring home your paperwork so start packing," I was speechless! That night, my prayers went something like "Okay, I surrender . . . I'm going, but I don't understand any of this so I'm hoping You let me in on what is really happening to me and why."

I don't know, but I'm guessing the Creator got a good chuckle out of it.

The day arrived. I was anxious, nervous, my emotions were running in circles. I stared out the window of the plane into the heavens asking God, "Please don't leave me now, You got me here . . . so please watch out for me."

I didn't speak to a soul on the plane, I only prayed, and kept imagining all the things that could go wrong; and what would I do if they did? I was excited, thrilled, and yet terrified all at the same time. As I made the dreaded walk up the terminal, I couldn't believe that I was there, so far from home, walking into unknown territory, both geographically and spiritually.

Then I saw her. It was Reba, Rudy's wife. Her eyes got big, her mouth dropped open, and I laughed out loud before saying, "Hey Reba." I was *not* what she was expecting. I had tried to warn them prior to my coming that although I may be of Cherokee descent, let's face it, I'm a "white girl" for all intents and purposes. The blonde hair and fair skin didn't just catch Reba off guard, it *threw* her off.

After getting my luggage, we made our way to Hisle, South Dakota. I still had not met Rudy, and my nerves were on edge. In all honesty, I was afraid, and kept thinking, "Lord, what I have gotten myself into?" Once there, I saw Rudy for the first time. When I looked into those deep brown-black eyes . . . the weight, the tension, and the fear that was like a cinder block on my chest lifted, disappeared into thin air. It was with that look . . . I saw, I knew, I relaxed.

Standing before me was a warrior of the Creator God. The love within him radiated outward and touched all those around him. It wasn't something someone could see with their eyes, but feel in their soul.

There were several people there. More were coming and going all the while, and the laughter of children was everywhere. It was a wonderful sound as the laughter of the children seemed to sparkle in the electrified air. As time went on I met several more children

Rudy and his dog, Thunder

and adults who I'm certain I will never forget. Rudy had spoken to them all before my arrival and told them who I was, why I was there, and asked them to speak freely to me. Otherwise, I'm quite certain they would not have otherwise. They would have considered opening up to a stranger betrayal to him.

Now keep in mind, I did know when I got there that I would be writing this book, I had only had begun to explore this knowledge a week or so prior to my arrival. When Rudy told me he wanted me to write his story, I was flabbergasted. He even tried to plant the seed in my head that it was my idea . . . I thought, "Oh no you don't . . . that's my trick, and it ain't working on me, Chief!"

After a day or two of thinking and praying about it, my answer came... I was out-numbered, out-witted, and out-ranked. The only thing for me to do was hold on tight for the ride of my life. The "dream team" from the spirit world was calling all the shots and I was just a tiny little player in this big game for which I didn't even know the rules. The only thing left to do was cinch the saddle up tight and pray this spirit horse didn't buck me off.

I've been around men all my life – it happens when you're the only girl in the family. One thing I've learned is that with the average man, he has one woman in his life he puts above all others, his mother. Rudy took me to meet his mother one night so I could sit down and chat with her and ask a few questions. There was just something about her... she has a way of drawing you in, spiritual charisma perhaps? I don't think she is aware of it, but when you meet her you just feel like you know her somehow – or maybe I just wanted to know her more. She had an energy about her, one that I could feel, and it was a good energy. My twinge of nervousness vanished when she said "Hello" to me, and once again, I relaxed. One word was all it took, and that beautiful smile; her eyes contained a love that my words cannot do justice. The energy surrounding her and the love in her eyes made me feel as if I had returned home after being gone for way too long. It was a new and strange feeling, like I had known her before... but there is no way I could have.

The following are a few questions I asked Mrs. Janis (Rudy's mom) and found myself fascinated while I listened to her soothing voice as she spoke.

Q: What was Rudy like as a child? Mischievous?
A: Serious.
Q: His siblings?
A: Six children altogether, four boys and two girls. All are Christians, but all don't follow the Native path as Rudy does. I'm proud of my children and love them all the same . . .
Q: Tell me about the day Rudy told you he was to be a Holy Man . . .
A: I was concerned about the criticisms of others . . . I called him a Prayer man.

She told me about some of the abuse Rudy was subjected to as a child. It was horrendous. Not by a direct family member, rather a woman his father had married some time after his parents had divorced. The stepmother would lock him away, refuse to feed him, but never missed an opportunity to beat him. Life growing up for him during this time was pure hell. I felt the rumble of my own rage deep within which I had to pull the reins on and keep in check. It is this mistreatment and abuse as a small boy that more than likely lead to a rowdy teenager and young man, but we'll get to that later. As she spoke of how she took Rudy to a medicine man to interpret his dreams for him, I watched Rudy as I took my notes; his head was lowered, and I suspected the visual memories were vivid in his mind as she spoke.

"He had always had these . . . dreams," she said, "and they always came to pass." She told me of how she left him with the medicine man for two nights, and of how he returned three days later. This man had told Rudy what his dreams meant, and then warned him: "This life will be really hard, are you ready for that?"

Rudy told his mom when he got back home he was going to Green Grass, and he walked all the way there. It was there he met this man again. The man is known to Rudy as Uncle Arvol, and he is known to many others as Chief Arvol LookingHorse

I was hesitant to ask about Rudy's dad and I suppose she picked up on that. My eyes looked up slowly to meet hers, and much to my surprise, she looked at me, smiled, and said, "Rudy looks like his dad, but he was everybody's kid. Everybody loves him . . . a couple different ones have even adopted him." On the outside I smiled back at her and on the inside I was scratching my head wondering how could she have known what I was thinking? Somehow she had read my thoughts. How could this be?

As I was writing my notes as fast as I could, I remember wondering what words of wisdom she would share with me next. I didn't know or understand how she had tuned into my thought process, but . . . when I finally raised my eyes to meet hers, I could tell she had patiently waited on me to make eye contact again and I can still hear her soothing voice as she spoke these words. I don't think I'll ever forget them . . . "Always know your place. Always know you are never better than, or stronger than, Creator. And never . . . abandon your faith."

I did understand one thing at this point. I knew where Rudy had gotten that aura around him. He and his mother both had this warmth about them; a love that was so strong inside them one could literally feel it when close to them . . . it was calming to one's spirit to be near it.

I met several medicine men while at Sundance, and there are always a few who stand out, whether they mean to or not. One of those was John.

He was quiet around me for the most part, or more quiet than what I'm used to, anyway. He didn't talk much really . . . but I sensed right away that when he did speak, I'd better listen. He was telling me things I needed to know, teaching me in his own calm way. Now keep in mind, I had just met this man, I didn't know him on personal level . . . but at the same time he was allowing me to see and get to know him—not all "medicine men" do. I never heard him call himself a medicine man, but then . . . no real medicine man does.

John and Rudy are like brothers. I believe there is an unbreakable bond there, a loyalty, a kinship that is stronger than the two of them. There is a reason for it; this is how the Creator works when he wants certain people in your life, there is a reason for it. Do yourself a favor and go with it. Remember the quote from Mrs. Janis? "Know your place." We are not in control here. There is One much better and stronger, as she pointed out.

John knows this all too well. Since I arrived home, John has been true to his word, and has e-mailed a few of his thoughts. I'd like to share a few of those with you the reader:

"The people who don't believe Rudy, or believe in his cause, I think it has to do with his last name, and it shouldn't be that way. Spirituality is just that, and it shouldn't be judged by any man, but be accepted and be grateful for the help they seek in another who *is* chosen."

For Rudy, being a mix-blood has caused him a few issues, (as all mix-bloods can relate to) but only with certain people, not the Creator, or those that love Him. Rudy's mom is right, everybody loves him. Those who say negative things about him are learning they are wrong in what they speak, or they will learn soon enough. There appears to be some jealousy on the part of a few which does make one wonder – why not learn from him instead? Take a chance and speak to him as a man, one on one. I suppose there will always be those who spread lies and negativity, but by now they surely know, they have no power or direct effect on Rudy, or anyone, for that matter, unless one allows it. We all have the power within us, and one should never give their power away. God gives us all our own power, and this power can and should be used to keep the deceiver at bay.

Here is another quote from John:

"Rudy is who he is and it is *God* that chose him, *not* any man. When a man tells you, 'This man made me a medicine man' or 'I am a medicine man' then he is *not*. It is *God* who decides who He wants to use for HIS purposes . . . healing, sending messages, etc. . . . "

John refers to himself, and Rudy as "The Brothers Who Help Others." This is no exaggeration on his part – this is truth. Rudy has had ceremonies for those who are sick with AIDS, cancer, and other illnesses. The Creator healed them through using Rudy as "tool" or a "vessel." The average person may or may not understand this concept, but before you pass judgment, speak to your own Elders, preacher, priest, rabbi, or leader of a faith you lean towards. I'm certain they can help shed some light on this for you.

After these ceremonies, Rudy told each of the individuals to keep their doctor's appointment and have new test run. When they did this, they would call Rudy afterward, each one saying almost verbatim the same thing: "The doctor says he can't explain it, and he doesn't understand it, but the cancer (or AIDS or what ever the illness was) is gone according to the test." His final instructions to each one was to give thanks to the Creator God and to live their lives according to His word. These individuals are still healthy today.

Rudy is old school, and the Native ways of healing were taught to him by God, not by man or men. Although his Uncle Arvol did teach him many good things, Rudy gives all credit to the Creator for all he knows, and all he is able to do to help others. The ways of the Native people are indeed sacred, they are not for sale. That is not what this book is about: it is about a man named Rudy Escamilla; and about the Creator God who has chosen him to help His children, and to lead them back to one true God where they belong.

My education in spirituality during these eight days was . . . phenomenal. I thought I was doing fairly well in my own spirituality, but since I first became acquainted with Rudy I have learned more than I know how to express. Praying is not enough. Faith in the one True God on its own, is not enough. The Bible says something like "even the demons in hell know this is true and shudder." (James 2:19: *Thou believest that there is one God; thou doest well: the devils also believe, and tremble.*) There is so much more, so much more in order to have a deep, personal relationship with the Great Spirit. When our actions back up our words, things begin to happen. Your eyes begin to open; your ears begin to hear; your spirit begins to feel. It's as if you are awakening from being in a deep sleep and noticing things, smells, sights, sounds – and an abundance of other things you simply never noticed before. Colors become softer, or brighter, or deeper . . . all at the same time. Have you noticed the breeze has a smell? It will bring to you what was in its path. You cannot see the wind, only the results of it. You cannot reach out and touch it, yet you can feel it. You cannot catch it, but you can embrace it.

My friend and sister Rose Butler, who introduced me to Rudy, brought her husband Bryan with her. He said something to me that still stands out in my mind. It was one of those Oprah light bulb moments. His words are true and wise and I refer to them every now and again.

> *"The harder you hold on to something, the harder it is for Creator to help you. You have to do your part. It's never wrong not knowing . . . It's wrong in not doing what you learn."*
>
> *Bryan Butler*

There was a ceremony that had taken place at Rudy's house one night, which involved me to some degree, but . . . was much bigger than me. I've had some fairly serious health issues for quite some time. Rudy said, "I can help you with this, Creator told me to." Now I suppose many would be skeptical and I can't say I would blame them, if it was anyone other than Rudy saying this. But I had been put through it (putting it nicely) just to get to this point. By this time, I had stopped fighting it and had come to the realization it really was the Creator God in control of all around me . . . including Rudy. We had had a few conversations, and he had explained some things to me.

On Rudy's instructions, I spent the best part of day with John, listening and hanging on his every word. John spoke softly, taught gently, and he waited patiently as he watched me take in his words and try to file them away in the proper folders in my brain.

While I cannot share the details of what happened in the ceremony that took place later, I can tell you it changed my life. Truth . . . Rudy had spoken to me about being able to help my health issues, and Truth . . . was delivered. Things in that regard have indeed improved and are improving still.

While I'm grateful for this fact, the most important thing to me is my spiritual growth; and now that my health is better I can focus more on Creator and what He has in store for me. As Bryan Butler said, I have do my part now. Now what does that mean exactly? Well . . . I'm learning as I go.

Thankfully the Creator is a patient and loving God and is easing me into this.

It was great sitting down with Rudy and just talking . . . and then I started with the questions. When he speaks of the Creator he gets this gleam in his deep dark eyes that expose a joy some can only hope for. He lights up and comes to life. It was inspiring to see how he changed before me from this fairly quiet, somewhat serious grown man into a man with only a slight grin on his face; but those eyes – they almost danced with the eagerness of a young boy's excitement. This is how much he loves God. How refreshing and what a true inspiration. I found his answers to be simple, blunt, and very honest.

Q: Tell me the difference in the old Rudy, and the Rudy that now works for the Creator.
A: Now I love myself.
Q: Before you got your altar, what was most important to you?
A: Nothing . . . Myself . . . I was selfish.
Q: When you chose Christianity, did you feel as though you were turning your back on your culture?
A: No. I don't like the word culture, Indian ways are not a cult!
Q: Who were your mentors as a child?
A: Sitting Bull, Crazy Horse, Jesus . . .
Q: And now, as a man?
A: Without hesitation Arvol LookingHorse
Q: What do you believe to be the unforgivable sin?
A: Disobedience . . . it is a choice to obey or disobey.

Rudy and I talked more, and this warrior of God is quite impressive. He is a young man of 43 and has more wisdom tucked away in his head than some that have lived a lifetime. He openly shared some of his knowledge with me . . . but then, it just flows out him whenever he speaks. We talked into the wee hours, and my education in Spirit has grown considerably.

Another opportunity came when I could talk to Mrs. Janis again – Rudy's mother – but it was bittersweet as I listened. I enjoyed very much talking with her. She is the kind of woman who, if your mom has passed over, you would take into your heart for your own. She showed me a picture of Rudy's grandparents, and resemblance between him and his grandfather is remarkable. Rudy isn't the only person in his family with this background. His mom told me that his paternal grandmother was considered a Holy person. Rudy's dad is Mexican, and most Mexican people I have had the privilege of knowing are very spiritual.

Now, he didn't go from a small boy into manhood without getting a good taste of life. This meant he went through the same changes and trials like any young person does growing up, and many more severe ones than many others ever know. He also made his share of mistakes, and he admits this freely. He doesn't blame anyone other than himself for taking the wrong fork in the road and venturing down a path his family and Creator did not want for him during this time.

He drank, loved pretty girls, got into fights, and visited the local jail – for a stay that is. A weekend get-a-way of sorts, only it lasted for months. Even had room service, if bread and water counts for room service.

There was a battle going on, the one within himself . . . and the one with the Creator and Deceiver. Both wanted him. He had barely stayed one step ahead of the law; but one night, the law got him. They took him to a cell they said had been reserved just for him. I doubt the cop knew how right he really was.

It was decision time. It was a tug of war of good and evil and Rudy was in the middle; he was the rope they were tugging on. Rudy said he thought about many things that night, especially his children. He relived much of his past that night: the abuse at the hands of his stepmother; the beatings he had taken; the fact she refused to feed him going as far as to put a pad-lock on the refrigerator. Rudy's only refuge at that time was the dog house out back. Now, you know it's bad when a dog nudges his only bowl of food towards you and then backs away because even the dog realizes how hurt, beaten, and hungry you are.

Rudy's mom said, "This dog was his protector, his angel. A guardian angel sent by the Creator to watch over him, this angel just happen to have fluffy fur, a long tail, and canine teeth."

Sometimes he would steal food growing in peoples' gardens to keep up his strength; he knew it could be days before he got to eat again. He became quite good at rummaging through dumpsters for food or anything that would help him survive. He remembered also to give thanks for what he found.

One day while he was in the shower, his stepmother threw a big box of light bulbs in the shower with him and at him, and then stared at him hard. A powerful message to an eight year old boy. His dad was always at work when such abuse took place, but the truth was soon to be revealed to his dad. Rudy's older brother did rebel against this woman. His mother was too far away, scratching out a miserable life on the reservation with his younger siblings. With no car to get to her; no phones to call her for help, he did what he had to do, tried to help. He broke the padlock off of the refrigerator.

Rudy was too small for such action. She could not punish his older brother for defying her, so the abuse against Rudy not only continued, but became worse, much worse. She went as far as to tie him to the bumper of the car, leaving him out in the hot sun all day with no food, no water, and no shelter while she and her sister worked in the fields. They never even checked on him as far as to make sure he was okay.

No, instead . . . there were now two grown women attacking this young, small boy rather than one. His step mother and her sister did make time during the relentlessly long and hot day to throw huge dirt clods at him, causing him more pain, as if he had not suffered enough. It was as if this was a game to these two women. A demented, perverse, and brutal game where the ruthless behavior of these two women could reach some sort of sick and twisted form of satisfaction.

All day long he cried out in pain from the bruises of the beatings and the pains of hunger, but they ignored him. His cries were begging for help and relief even if his words were not. His words he kept silent, mouth closed other than the muffled gasp for air between cries. One day, it all became too much for him and he became terribly sick. His stepmother took him to the hospital, not out of concern, mind you, but fear. She wasn't afraid she had taken it too far; she was afraid of what Rudy's dad was going say and do. Thankfully, the doctors knew the cause of his injuries and fever and immediately and reported the truth: "child neglect." It was a long time in coming, but finally . . . he was being rescued. Or was he?

She left him all alone in the hospital four long days. During this time, Rudy prayed . . . and he prayed a lot. He asked the Creator to help him, and he was let out of the hospital one day before his dad returned home. Imagine that.

He began sleeping in parks, continued raiding gardens, doing what he had to to simply stay alive. "Anything," he thought, "anything was better than going back so this woman could hurt him even more."

She enjoyed humiliating him and did so every chance she got. She forced him to wear a dress one day and laughed at him. If that wasn't enough, she made him get out of the car wearing the dress for all to see . . . adults as well as his friends. The physical, mental, and emotional anguish this woman continued to force upon this boy had not only taken a toll, but had reached beyond that of any human being, let alone a small child.

Finally, one day in school, the teacher told him to take his sweater off. She knew by his body language something was wrong, terribly wrong. When he did as instructed and removed the sweater, slowly, painfully . . . she saw all the markings, the bruising, the welts from fresh lashings, the cuts into his skin. Thankfully, this teacher was at the right place at the right time or this would have continued. The teacher contacted the family and his dad kicked his stepmother out the next day. I can not imagine the horror and the anger Rudy's mother must have felt, as well as the disgust.

In that cell the realization came that the choice he made this night was not just a choice for himself. The woman he was married to at the time had made her choice as well, Rudy was now the sole caretaker of the young ones . . . his children. After being led down memory lane of his own childhood, he made his choice, and he chose the Creator. He would walk the Red Road, the Sacred Road, and do his best to make a better life for his children than he had.

Now fighting battles was nothing new to Rudy, and he wasn't afraid of it. He had had to fight his entire life and he had become good at it. What he was in for now, however, was a new kind of battle, one he could not simply punch, shoot, or steal his way through. No, this was different; this time he had to take a backseat and give all control over to the Creator; He would be the one doing any fighting that needed to be done from this day forward, not Rudy.

Rudy has had dreams all his life, the kind of dreams that come true. This is why his mother sent him to his Uncle Arvol as a child. His uncle had warned him then, that life being dedicated to the Creator would be hard; and he was about to learn how hard. This was a new beginning for him, and the path for him was being prepared while he sat alone in that jail cell. Many things were about to be revealed to him, and much sooner than he expected. Although the confines of his cell were growing smaller by the day, he had one opportunity for relief, albeit a small one, and he signed up for the Drum Circle that met every Wednesday. This was a relaxation for him, but not enough to forget where he was – jail. Nothing was enough to make him forget that – or so he thought.

His new path was being prepared for him by the Creator. This new path he knew would by no means be an easy one to walk, but there was one thing for sure, it was better than being locked up.

The day before he was released from jail, he lost his temper, and his cell mate pretended to be asleep during what happened next. He was angry with God and he yelled "Where have you been? Why didn't you come?" Rudy did not hear the answer he was seeking . . . not at that moment anyway, but the wait was a short one. Still angry . . . he cried. He cried hard and his prayers continued until he fell asleep. Although asleep, his prayer had now become a conversation between himself and God . . . one that continued while he slept. It was during this conversation Creator said to him: "Stay on the Red Road. . . . " Then Rudy smiled at me and quoted Black Elk:

"In church they talk About God; in Spirituality, you talk to God . . ."

Sometimes it may take a heartache, or a day of crying, or even a trip to jail for us to stop and listen to what the Creator has wanted to share with us. If He wants our attention, He will get it.

Sometimes, He may have a message for someone that they really need to hear. This time, that someone was Rudy, and the message was meant to save his life . . . and it did. That has been thirteen years ago now. He has run his own Sundance three years in a row and has danced at Green Grass at Arvol LookingHorse's Sundances as well as participated by dancing in nine other Sundances.

Rudy says Arvol is still his mentor to this day. He admires and respects him a great deal. They got together only three months ago and spent some time with each other, and when I left South Dakota, Rudy was leaving in a couple days to go see him again. While Rudy has several mentors, Arvol, of course, also Sitting Bull, and Crazy Horse, he says the most important mentor and one he loves the most is Jesus Christ. Rudy, unlike others, has learned how to talk to his mentor, Jesus, and to do so in such a way that Jesus talks back. Rudy doesn't waste time or energy on skeptics; he simply goes forward in his own personal way of worship. It's pretty awesome speaking to the Creator, and the only thing better and more exciting is when He answers you.

He, Creator, will talk to those who seek Him out with a sincere spirit. He will teach you, guide you, forgive you – and all because He loves you.

That night, the visions had only begun. His trips down memory lane were extremely visual and as real as if he were living it all over again. In a very real sense, I suppose he was.

Rudy was born in Nebraska, yet he lived and was raised on the Pine Ridge prisoner of war camp #434, better known these days as a reservation. Growing up as fast and hard as he did, gave him the old Mafioso "tough guy" mentality. The young ones today refer to it as "gangsta" life. Living this way meant you had to be prepared to defend yourself at any given moment, be it by fist or gun. Rudy admits he lead this lifestyle to the fullest, and his vision made him relive it all again.

Rudy was a man full of anger and resentment through those years. In his 20's the gangsta life had overtaken him. He drank, and he drank a lot. Fist fighting was just a tease to get the evening off to a good start. Prejudice was . . . a vile and nasty addition to all his other gangsta qualifications, and it made him cringe a little when telling me about it. One night it went a step further when he shot a man. Beating people up was not only expected, but a pleasure. And yet now, he was having to watch all this happen, watch himself doing all these wrongs like he was watching a movie of himself and knowing the Creator was watching it with him. He was embarrassed and felt ashamed.

Rudy prayed and prayed and said to the Creator, "Put me where you want me, teach me, I want to live Your will the way You want me to." Rudy had gone to all denominations in the past, but this night the Creator showed him he was go the Native way. To follow the Red Road. Imagine if you can, going to sleep living out fully the gangsta life, and wake up working for God.

Rudy was released from jail and in court the charges against him were dropped. He has been on this journey, a man of God ever since. He has never wavered from it.

In talking with Rudy, he hesitated and said: "You know, before I went to jail . . . I was drinking a lot. I was on the streets and one day while standing on a bridge, I began to watch the panhandlers.

"They would go to the Labor Force and get a job working one day. Earn just enough money to buy a bottle, get drunk, and then start over the next day. That was their life, that was all they did, all they had, it was what they had become."

I asked him, "You were drinking too right?" His honesty is always forthcoming, not missing a beat he said, "Yes, I can remember being hung-over and standing on this bridge watching. Watching all these people who were in the same place I was in – hungover and looking . . . looking for that next buzz and wondering where their next drink would come from."

Rudy said while on that bridge he began to wonder about other things. Things he had not wondered until that moment, "What do I want to do with my life?" He went on to tell me of the depression that took him over, the suicidal thoughts . . . especially if he was drunk or drinking.

During this time he openly admits he became hard hearted, he said and did mean things, awful things. He was prejudiced; he judged others based on skin color as well as other things; and people around him who in his mind, at least at that time, weren't good enough. He got into fights, lost more than one girlfriend, and was just an all around unhappy man. Then he would drink again. The drinking side of him came to an abrupt halt when he was arrested, but the depression and anger only festered like sore. He was, as he put it, "full of self-pity, having a pity party."

No one came to see him, no one would talk to him; except one man, the pastor of a church by the name of Donnie Williams. Rudy and Mr. Williams talked, and this did help Rudy some but it still did not fill the void. Donnie asked him what he wanted to do with his life. This question ate at him. He wanted answers, and decided the only way to get them, was to ask the One that had the answers. He'd been poor, sick, lonely, and alone . . . and now, he was a broken man. Things had to change.

Once he talked to the Creator and said, "Put me where you want me" . . . he went to many different churches of all denominations. He knew none were for him, but he went anyway. Rudy is a Christian, but he follows the Red Road. There are those that say the two don't mix, Christianity and the Red Road, and there are others who have done it, or are doing it, and have done it for years. Then of course, there are those who do and just don't admit to it. They even go as far as to criticize it on the social networks. Then, they will go to a meeting, a public tribal council meeting, for example, only for someone there to record them praying in Jesus's name on video and later put it on YouTube.

Rudy was looking for other medicine men he could learn from, and he wanted very much to do a ceremony that is called "going on the hill." There he would be doing a lot of praying. He would need to go in under another a medicine man to do this. There weren't any who were willing to help him. Several made fun of him, told him he was Mexican not Lakota. The fact his mother is a full blood Lakota mattered not to those judging him. An uncle rejected him and refused to teach him. He was of his own flesh and blood family. Rudy was hurt by this, and angered . . . but he refused to give up.

In reality it only made him more determined than ever because he knew The Medicine Man, The Holy Man, The Haoka of all Haokas was guiding him. He told of when he spoke to his mother about it. Being the loving mother she is, she said "Forget about them Rudy, go to the One that has the power to make this work for you." Rudy returned to one man he had been to before, an uncle. This time though, his uncle had a different attitude and he put Rudy on the hill. They were smoking the pipe and Rudy was the last one to share his pipe. When his uncle, Leonard Crow Dog handed the pipe back to him, he said: "Protect this pipe, everything is going to come true."

Rudy knew and understood his uncle was referring to his dreams. A brief time later, Rudy and his Uncle Arvol were talking, he shared with him what Crow Dog had said. Arvol spoke to him and said, "Take care of your headdress and shirt like you do your pipe." Rudy understood the unspoken message, and did as he was told. Rudy's knowledge was growing remarkably fast. Some speak of tradition – but that is all they do, speak words. Being traditional means taking care of family first. It means keeping the mind free and sober, and one's thoughts in prayer.

"The women, the way they dress, they are looking for a man," he said. "That is not tradition. The men, they drink and carouse . . . that is not tradition. Putting the Creator God first, that is tradition. Taking care of family or other members of the tribe that cannot take care of themselves, that is tradition. The Ultimate Spirit belongs to all things, to all people, to the world. He is to be honored. That, my sister," he said to me, "is tradition."

He quoted his grandmother's words to me, Hazel Thunder Bull. "Tradition, Rudy, is kindness, humility, to take good care of your family . . . this is what it means to be the leader of a great nation."

Walking through "the valley of the shadow of death" had become home to Rudy Escamilla during his gangsta days; but he now took his knowledge, his past, and put it to good use so he could reach others who were still living that life. Once he had taken the steps to get to where he needed to be, he took to the streets he knew so well . . . he went back to his old hangouts. Only this time he was armed with the word of God, not a gun. This time it was genuine love his lips he spoke, not anger. And this time, his backup was the Creator Himself, not a group of revenge seeking, hate filled, rebellious drunks. Rudy felt great.

His was healthy, he was clean and sober, and he never once doubted who his Partner with him was, or if he was protected. Batman had Robin, the Lone Ranger had Tonto, and Rudy . . . well, the one true God now had Rudy by his side. God has many names. In Lakota, he is called Tunkasila. Many call him Creator, Great Spirit, The Great Mystery. Each tribe may use a different name, as each religion has its own name for Him.

Rudy had been changed even more than he realized. When he looked at the people, from all walks of life, he no longer felt the anger or disgust he felt only a few months ago. Rather he felt love for them, and he realized they were as lost as he was just a short time ago. He wanted to reach them, inside deep ... beyond the flesh and bones and shake their spirit awake. He refused to accept the answer no, and would always leave them with the words, "I'll pray for you; and when your ready, give me a call, I'll be there for you." Many things have happened since that time, and now many seek him out, asking for help, for guidance and mostly ... for prayer.

John Stand By Ear describes Rudy pretty good in the following quote:

"I had seen him cry and heard him cry not only in sweats, but at Sundances too. He is a man but has Love, Compassion, Care, Understanding and Humbleness for all. He doesn't judge others in any way, shape, or form, or for whatever reason they have to seek help through him. He is willing to help."

Rudy prays more than any one who I personally know, and that is saying a lot; because I know some folks who pray a lot. If a person has had a dream where the Creator talked to them, gave them a message of some kind, or had a vision, it is not something that "I" could explain to them. I think it is something one must experience for themselves. I know this to be true for me, and I know it is true for Rudy. Dreams and visions are nothing new to him, and the message is not always an easy one as far as what the Creator may ask of us. Rudy knows this all too well.

Rudy was given the "prophecies" and told to "tell them to the people," and some of them have already come to pass. These are those prophecies:

(1) Many false prophets will be revealed, because the truth will reveal them all.

(2) If you take away the gift that God gave to you, "life" ... if you take your life or commit suicide, you will go to a place where everything that you can think of that is bad or evil is all there and no matter how many prayers that are said for you, it won't help you. There is no coming back from there. You'll stay there forever, for eternity. You never get to see your family members or your relatives that left before or after you.

(3) These are the times of great purification, not the end of the world. No one knows when the end of the world will be, just the Creator God and Him alone.

(4) There will be tornadoes, floods, earth quakes and droughts of many kinds and there will be a massive famine that will sweep across the land like the wind.

(5) There will be a wide disease epidemic that will go across the land like the wind.

(6) The Maya Indians predicted that the volcanoes will erupt – that's what they thought because that was the only kind of explosions that they were used to seeing in those times. My relatives, there will be a bright light in the west and will leave behind a massive mushroom cloud and seconds later the same exact thing in the east and the light will burn everything in its path, then our country will be invaded by foot soldiers from the north and south.

(7) Rapid City, South Dakota and many other cities like it will be the first to be invaded; all residents and people caught within the cities will be held as prisoners of war. No one will be allowed to leave these cities once they've been invaded.

(8) America will be invaded by two other countries, and there will be war here in our homeland. Food will be hard to get a hold of and the water won't be drinkable due to the poisoning to the water systems.

(9) There will be a new law of the land and any other law will be a threat.

(10) A lot of true spiritual leaders, the ones that were hand picked by the Creator God, will be a threat to this new law and will be hunted down by the officers of the U.N.I.T, United Nations International Treaties, and without any proof of wrongdoing, they will be shot.

(11) Common man has been chasing after the things of man instead of the spiritual ways of our Creator God, and our children are suffering because of it and are lost due to the lack of spiritual direction in life.

(12) If you are living a homosexual life and the spirit happens to take you, you will go to a dark place where evil is always present, a place where hardship and cries never end, this place is in the northwest.

(13) A place of survival has already been chosen and a man that will lead the people through this storm has also already been chosen.

(14) Don't take these warnings lightly! Many will hear these and

will prepare and that will be good. Many will hear these warnings and won't prepare, but they've been warned.

(15) I encourage you to prepare yourselves like our ancestor did when they prepared for the winter and pray, because their prayers can't come from anywhere else but from deep within. Love and take care of one another.

(16) A portion of California will fall off into the water and will cause a big tsunami, Hawaii and Japan will be no more. The entire east coast will fall into the water and disappear and be no more.

(17) These are some of the ways that the Creator God is cleaning the bad out of the world in which we live. I'm hoping that the people will see the bad and try to change and become better human beings.

(18) On November 18, 2008, at 11:15 AM. I spoke on KILI Radio on the Pine Ridge Reservation about these warnings and I stated as proof "a sign" of what I'm telling you, there will be tornadoes during the winter season until all the prophecies come to pass. Since three days after I stated this, there's been tornadoes during the winter season since that day. But still, people don't believe, just weak in faith, they need a bigger sign. Well sorry, that's the only one God allowing us.

(19) I've been posting these warnings since last year, on paper, radio, and verbally and others have spoken of them while talking about me, I don't mind that because the word's getting out. A man came from the stars and told me to warn the people and help them, but he also said that there will be disbelief and doubt, but I warned the people like the star nations asked me too. Our ancestors came from the star nations. So remember, if you are not preparing, I Warned You!

(20) Again, my name is Rudy Escamilla and my Lakota name is Wocekiya Gluh Mani, I live in Hisle, South Dakota on the Pine Ridge Reservation and I am a spirit healer, "Wanagi Wapiya Wicasa." So if you have any questions about anything else that the star nation told me, feel free to stop by and visit. I'm always home to Hece Tu Yelo Mitakuye Oyasin

(21) You all have heard my words. Some of my dreams of prophecies have already taken place and some are taking place as we speak and some are still yet to come. I warn you, because I love you and I want what is best for you; but just remember this . . . any other survival shelter made anywhere else will fall and be destroyed; the

chosen survival place is Hisle, South Dakota, and the Creator said he will provide water and food for those who are here when the time comes . . . .

How does one prepare? Prepare by stocking up on food, water, medical supplies . . . many can go to Hisle, they are close enough, but many can not, that is true. Preparation through prayers is always available. If humans start living life for God, perhaps He will show mercy on all of us, and lifestyle changes and beliefs would be a gesture of "good faith" in the eyes of God – but only God can answer if that will be enough.

Here is a direct quote from Rudy, one he has shared with others many times. I hope you will take it heart:

> "Holy men are very rare, and very hard to find. They are blessed and chosen by the Creator God, and when they speak . . . their words are sacred. Those that curse these men, God curses them. And those that bless these ones . . . God blesses them; because they have a direct connection To and are protected By God. These kind of men are born into the world for that purpose, 'to be holy,' and were holymen before entering the world(s), and the man-made ones are the ones who prayed to become one after they've been already born into the world and these men don't have the direct connection to God, but only to his helpers . . . but the thing about this is, God is the one who decides who is and who isn't, and my advice is not to appoint oneself into that position of authority because it can be dangerous and weighs heavy against God. Some people who do self-appoint themselves, 'self-proclaim,' most of them are sickly and most of their family members are gone. I guess my advice on this is to 'wait until God himself tells you that he chooses you' . . ."

Itancan Wocekiye Gluha Mani
Chief Walks With Prayers

Being a "holy man," be it a Lakota man, or men from other Tribes or Nations or races . . . is not to be taken lightly. Not everyone believes the way Rudy does, he knows this. But those who show contempt by bearing false witness against one that is hand picked and chosen by God are literally playing with fire. The prophecies that Rudy has stated so many times to others, and that you have now read – believe them or don't believe them. I will ask, though, what does he have to gain by making it up? He will make no profit from it. He is not now, nor has he ever, asked for or tried to "recruit followers." And he would be losing his position with the Creator and throwing away any chances of making into Heaven.

He asks no man (mankind) for anything. He is held accountable to the most high God, and no matter what your personal beliefs may be, know this . . . God Is Watching! There will be a day of reckoning for us all. I heard a man say once:

> "Does the moon say to the stars, 'You owe me,' or does the sun say to the earth, 'You owe me'? No, they simply do what they were created to do. This is what a holy man does as well. They were created for this purpose, then born into this world with one purpose – to serve the Creator God. There is no need for the sea to ask the clouds for rain; the clouds send the rain when it is needed. There is no need for the forest to ask the rivers for a drink of its bountiful waters, the rivers' water were made for this purpose."

It's all part of His plan, and this plan was designed long before we humans came along. And what a mess we have made of things.

Through the ages, the Creator has sent many of these holy men to help us, teach us, guide us.

Do we listen?

Do you?

By the looks of the world today, the greed, the hatred, the crimes against humanity . . . we obviously have not been listening. Perhaps every generation says, "The time is at hand." Was it then? Is it now? Since only the Creator Himself knows the day and hour the end for us all will come, I ask you . . . is it a chance you're willing to take? Are you willing to turn your back on the Creator God that gave you life? Only you can answer this. If you are not sure what to believe, I encourage you to ask for guidance same from the Creator.

If you don't believe in Christ Jesus, that He is indeed the Son of the Creator God, I'm asking you to reconsider that thought. The

God that Created All Things also created some of the "men" others now worship and call their god. Would you not be better to put your faith in Him? To those that say, "prove this true," I respond with, "prove to me it isn't . . . "

If I am wrong, if Rudy is wrong, if Arvol LookingHorse is wrong, if Billy Graham is wrong, what have we lost? Nothing, and at least these men lead a good life. But those who believe not, if you are wrong . . . you have lost it all! And for what? Money? Prestige? Lust? Could eternity in hell really be a price worth paying? How can anyone walk this earth for any length of time and not believe a hell worse than this exist? Does it not get worse in this world with each passing day?

For believers, it doesn't come as easy as the non-believers may think. We all have trials and tribulations; it's just that not all of us are willing to pass on them for temporary fix. And this is temporary. Our lives, this earth, everything you see and don't see . . . it is all temporary. All will be made new, fresh, and clean. There will be no such thing as hate, or greed, or power, or control over others. The days of mankind tormenting mankind will cease forever. There will be no more tears, no more pain, no more heartache, death or dying . . . if another God could offer me a deal as sweet as that one, or better, I'd consider taking it. But they can't! How do I know? Because they would have done it by now! Think about that for a minute . . . The Creator offers us all what we could ever hope for, and all we have to do is choose Him over the world. What has anyone else ever offered you?

Rudy had gone to all denominations in the past. Of course, the deceiver, the liar of all liars, the evil one, Satan may offer you a deal. But in exchange for what? Your soul, and eternity in hell with him. So weigh that one out in your mind for a moment, "all things good" versus "all things evil and painful" – what do you think? We all have to make a stand and choose sooner or later. If we do not, you are leaving your fate in the hands of the dealer. Surely we all know by now that "betting against the house" isn't the wisest move to make.

In this case, there are two dealers, Good and evil. At which table are you sitting? Cards are dealt, it's your turn to bet . . . I'm sitting at the table of the Creator and I'm betting it all. (I've read the book, I know who wins . . .) What are you willing to bet? What are you willing to loose? Because at the evil one's table, Nobody Wins! Not even him . . . not even the house dealer.

Another medicine man who was there, was "Shrek," a new nickname, not using his real name at his request in this book. Shrek is a good-sized man who is the jolly sort, but not all that talkative unless you engage him. We spoke several times and he stated a couple things that Rudy had taught me. For example:

> *"Any man that tells you he is a medicine man, he is Not. And if they ever ask for money, leave. Prayer is for free. The Creator does not charge us anything to speak to Him, and no man has the right to do so either."*

Shrek was always smiling, whether he was talking about God, his brothers, Rudy, John, and the rest . . . or simply working on his truck. When I learned the story of when he and Rudy first met, I couldn't help but laugh a little bit.

"I was afraid to meet you," Shrek said to Rudy. "I've heard the stories that you are powerful and strong in what you believe. And I watched you get your 100 piercings."

Rudy asked why he was afraid to met him, and Shrek said, "I thought you were spooky, but . . . I've changed my mind on that. You're not spooky . . . you're just crazy!"

There was a ceremony while I was there, along with many sweats and, of course, the Sundance itself. I can't share everything with you, but I can tell you enough to make you want to learn more. Not to learn "how to become Native," but rather how to follow the Creator in a more spiritual way, as opposed to following "religion" or religious dogma – ideals of men mixed with some scripture. Be content with what God made you: He made you who and what you are; the color, race you are; and He did so for a reason. Embrace that about yourself and strive for a better way to serve to Him.

It took many days, a lot of people, and whole lot of hard work to prepare for Sundance and all that goes with it. There is some down time too, and that is when my best lessons came. I was told stories of their ancestors that had me on the edge of my seat. I could hardly wait to hear the next words flow from the mouths of my mentors.

I learned much of the history of the Sundance, the different steps taken, and the reasons behind them. I'll share as much as I can with you. However, spiritualism is very sacred to the Lakota people. It is not to be used or abused or – especially – sold for profit. Remember the scripture where Jesus got angry for turning His house into a "den of thieves"? Mark 11:17: "And He taught, saying unto them, Is it not written, My house shall be called of All Nations the house of prayer? But ye have made it a den of thieves."

A few have gotten away from this through the years, but most have not. I respect the Creator and love Him; and for that reason, I will not betray His Lakota children, my friends, and my mentors, and now my family. I will not betray my Father in heaven . . . for He is their Father also.

In the first few days, there is a time all gather in their cars and trucks and go out looking for what is referred to as the tree of life. This tree will be put in the center of the Sundance grounds. I don't think I can say much more than that really, other than what a wonderful time I had watching, listening, and learning. The obvious closeness of all that participated, the laughter, and the respect and love shown to one another flowed freely. Respect was shown to the earth and to the tree before it was ever cut. It is what some may call "the little things" that stood out to me the most. Your average man, non-Native man when he wants to go out and cut a tree . . . he just cuts it. It's done. Not so with those taught the deepest respect of everything the Creator provides for us all on this earth. There is a ritual procedure, if you will, that is to be followed, and in all things done, one is to give thanks to the Creator for making it possible.

For any those of you who are not Native American, and you're thinking this is the way for the "Indians," the "brown man only" . . . I'll take this opportunity to remind you that Christ also was a "brown man." He was not a white man. Hebrew is a religion, not a race. He was Hebrew. Jews are of many races.

For those that have had their heads stuck in the dogma of "religious" faith so long that they don't really know what it means to be spiritual, please read the following scripture:

> "But the natural man receiveth not the things of the Spirit of God; for they are foolishness to him; neither can he know them, because they are spiritually discerned."
>
> I Corinthians 2:14

With the tree cut, each man having taken his turn in the chopping of it; "the tree of life" it is called, (and no one passed out from the grueling Dakota heat, not even me) we returned to the ceremonial grounds. What did each man do after cutting the tree? He helped to carry it to where it was to be stood up. The tree was raised in place in the proper way. The heat was overpowering and weakened the body and the mind, but that could not detour the mission at hand. Sage and cedar were burned, and prayer was offered to Creator in thanksgiving for the tree that was chosen. So despite the heat, there was a peacefulness that covered the land and the small group of us there.

The smiles of joy and grateful hearts were exposed for only those of us there and God Himself to see, and all looked forward to the ceremony to come, and the purpose behind it, the Sundance.

Once we returned to Rudy's, Shrek took some time to speak with me. Our chats were fairly short since he was working a lot, but he always made time for me when he could. When I asked him how long he had had his altar, he told me five years. I asked him how he came to choose this path; he quickly pointed out, "It chose me."

While Shrek is a Christian, I asked if it surprised him that some refused the same path that he and Rudy walk. "No, not with the boarder school era and genocide." (For which Christians were responsible.) I said, "Tell me one thing about spirituality you felt was the most the important," and I was not disappointed in how this man thinks. He quickly said, "The children's spirituality."

I asked, "What advice would you give me, or someone like me?" He smiled and said, "Don't ever stop." We talked of all the negative things that happen daily, be it something on the news, or everyday life for the average person. He said, "It's natural for humans to see the negative first. It takes more effort to see the good." As he was pouring a cup of coffee, I said "Shrek, if you could have one prayer answered today, what it be?" Without blinking an eye he said, "Unity for all the Lakota people."

He watched me carefully as I scribbled my notes as quickly as I could while I was trying to process his answers. I had a question in mind, but I was hesitant about a second too long in asking, I suppose, when he said to me with only his eyes smiling, "Be humble . . . Creator will take care of the rest for you." I sighed a bit of relief at that statement and was thankful for his response, yet wondered . . . "has he been hanging out with Mrs. Janis? How do they know what I'm thinking?" It didn't exactly seem fair in one sense, and yet was a great relief in another.

Knowing my friends – even if no one else – will read this, I asked Shrek, "To those who read this book, and want to learn more about the ways of the Lakota, what would say to them?" His answer took a more serious tone, but it was still gentle and he said, "Respect our ways enough to learn them, and learn them correctly . . . and always treat us and others with respect."

I was watching the children play, listening to their laughter, and got a couple of minutes to talk to Joseph, Reba's nephew. He was learning a new song for the ceremony coming up, so our visit was a short one. He told me he has known Rudy, Uncle Rudy, for eight years. He said he began to trust Rudy around the time he, Joseph, hit puberty. He said it was about the time of Rudy's first prediction. "Something just clicked," he said. He smiled giving a slight chuckle and said to me, "This guy is for real!"

He then returned his attention to Rudy, and the two sang a song together to make sure Joseph knew it well enough to sing during ceremony that night.

The time had finally come for the ceremony that would include me, at least to a small degree. I have to say it was the most wonderful night of my life. It has changed me forever, and for this I am so grateful to the Creator that I cry every time I relive it. Joseph, and the sweetest young man named Jamison, Shrek and Jonathan played the drums and were the singers. I knew each voice as I listened, and enjoyed it a great deal. Then it changed. It was no longer "just my friends" singing. Now I know who was there mind you, I was there too . . . I saw them all. But within a matter of minutes, it sounded like there were One Hundred voices singing that prayer song! I was stunned, shocked . . . and I loved it! Now if you have ever been to a Yuwipi, you know what I'm talking about.

If you have not, all I can say is heaven will be fabulous! Beyond fabulous, beyond awesome, and I can hardly wait. I get so excited thinking about it.

I talked to Rudy a few minutes ago, and he gave me this scripture:

Fear thou not; for I am with thee: be not dismayed; for
I am thy God: I will strengthen thee; yea, I will help thee;

> *yea, I will uphold thee with the right hand of my righteousness.*
>
> *Isaiah 41:10*

That night during ceremony, I didn't even know about this scripture and I felt the truth in these words emerge. I have never felt closer to God as I did that night and many nights since. I have never known such joy, such peace, or such overwhelming love. I felt all these things in my heart, mind, body, and soul. This is how it feels when God is right there with you and "allowing" you to know it. No one will ever convince me otherwise . . . I was there, I know what I felt. I can't speak for anyone else, or speak on anything that took place, but until my dying day, I will stand by this statement. Yes, even old Christians can learn, and I sincerely hope many do. Having one's faith "renewed" in such a loving, grand, and yet humble way can and will change one's life.

For any that doubt if Rudy Escamilla is real, I challenge you to go to sweat with him or go to ceremony with him. Rather than pass judgment, which you have no right to do, go to him. Talk to him, one on one, step up, be the better person, and learn rather than judge. As Rudy has told me and countless others, its not about religion, its about spirituality.

> *For to be carnally minded is death; but to be spiritually minded is life and peace.*
>
> *Romans 8:6*

We cheat ourselves when we allow mankind's "religion" rather than God's spirituality to guide us, to dictate our path. If you have allowed this to happen, take your power back and trust in the Creator to guide you instead. If any really knew Rudy, they would have heard him say these very things. Rudy is not a hard man, but a very loving man. However, he will not waver from the word of God. So if you read a scripture you're not too crazy about, one that does not suite your purpose, Rudy will not sugarcoat it and hold your hand for you. He will tell you straight up truth . . . so be sure you really want the truth before you ask him for it.

In the prophecies the Creator gave him for example, there are a few people that don't want to hear, or they want to argue the point. Lets look at #2 for example:

(2) If you take away the gift that God gave to you, "life" . . . if you take your life or commit suicide, you will go to a place where everything that you can think of that is bad or evil is all there and no matter how many prayers that are said for you, it won't help you. There no coming back from there. You'll stay there forever, for eternity. You never get to see your family members or your relatives that left before or after you. . . . If you love your children talk to them.

You may not believe these words, however they are true.

> *Oh that I might have my request; and that God would grant me the thing that I long for!*
> *Even that it would please God to destroy me; that he would let loose his hand, and cut me off!*
> *Then should I yet have comfort; yea, I would harden myself in sorrow: let him not spare; for I have not concealed the words of the Holy One.*
>
> *Job 6:8–10*

and Job 14:13–14:

> *O that thou wouldest hide me in the grave, that thou wouldest keep me secret, until thy wrath be past, that thou wouldest appoint me a set time, and remember me!*
> *If a man die, shall he live again? all the days of my appointed time will I wait, till my change come.*

Life is not a "possession" of man's, but it is a gift from God, and He alone is the true "owner" of life. It is His to give and His to take away. God has ordained a natural process for the ending of this life and the beginning of the next. This is His domain solely and the Creator alone is responsible for it, for Life is Sacred. This is not what family and friends of one that has taken their own life want to hear, I understand that. But no one has the power to change the word of God other than God Himself.

Not all believed Rudy when he warned of the tornadoes. He started telling of these things back in 2008. In the year 2011, there were over 300 tornadoes in the States alone. That in itself is enough for me step back and "think about it".

(16) A portion of California will fall off into the water and will cause a big tsunami, Hawaii and Japan will be no more. The entire east coast will fall into the water and disappear and be no more.

Remember the tsunami in Japan? No one believed him then either, until the day it happened.

Now for the one that brings the most controversy . . .

(12) If you are living a homosexual life and the spirit happens to take you, you will go to a dark place where evil is always present, a place where hardship and cries never end, this place is in the northwest.

God's plan for marriage is for a man and woman. Genesis 2:24. Anything else distorts the oneness He intended for sexual union between man and woman, and defies childbirth. In the Old Testament, homosexual behavior which does include lesbianism, was forbidden. It is considered "unclean" and cannot be tolerated by a Holy God. If He were to tolerate it, He would Not be Holy.

> *Therefore shall a man leave his father and his mother, and shall cleave unto his wife: and they shall be one flesh.*

The Creator offers those that have lived this lifestyle or simply participated in it mercy and forgiveness. (I Corinthians 6:9–11).

> *Know ye not that the unrighteous shall not inherit the kingdom of God? Be not deceived: neither fornicators, nor idolaters, nor adulterers, nor effeminate, nor abusers of themselves with mankind,*
> *Nor thieves, nor covetous, nor drunkards, nor revilers, nor extortioners, shall inherit the kingdom of God.*
> *And such were some of you: but ye are washed, but ye are sanctified, but ye are justified in the name of the Lord Jesus, and by the Spirit of our God.*

Both the Old Testament and New Testament refuse the possibility of excusing homosexual behavior for biological reasons. Therefore, it is a choice . . . You choose God's way for you to live, or live a live of sin and risk death in the midst of this sin.

If you choose to believe the deceiver's lies, if you can convince yourself that "God is wrong" . . . then that is on you. Being one of "two spirits" as those of many Native tribes and nations refer it, is not acceptable to God and His Holy word says it is an abomination. If you are not happy with this, talk to Creator about. These are not my words, or Rudy's . . . it says these things in God's Word. And only the Creator God has the power to offer forgiveness for a sin against Him. What I may think is irrelevant – you don't have to please me, or Rudy, or any preacher – but if you go against God, you will also answer to God.

As the hot sun began to lower in South Dakota, I thought of all I had learned. I read through my notes, smiled . . . but I wanted to learn so much more. Gazing out over the rolling hills, the sparseness of trees made me think of home, and although I missed my husband and dogs . . . I wanted more of what I was learning. I could not get enough; the more I learned, the more I wanted. That is only part of the love God shares with us: the more we open up to Him, the more He will allow us to take in and experience. I couldn't help but wonder if it was this way for Rudy when he started working for the Creator, and even before with his visions . . . always wanting more.

Everything that was happening around me had much more meaning, had more purpose than the average person could possibly know. The day we all went together for the chopping of the "tree of life," for example. This tree was not chosen randomly, as one might expect. It was explained to me this tree "offered itself" to be given, to be used in the Sundance ceremony; it had given itself for the Creator. This tree was treated with respect because of this. There was prayer offered, cedar burned, and thanks were given for this tree before the men ever took the ax to it – a valuable lesson that was repeated again and again. One must always give thanks to the Creator for everything in our life, no matter how small it may seem to some; all we have . . . all that we have been given, is a gift and only God has the power and ability to give these gifts.

Not all receive them either. I mean think about it, if a person never gives thanks for anything, as opposed to one that gives thanks for everything, which one will receive the most blessings? Blessings come in many forms; to grasp the true concept one must go about it from a spiritual stand point, not a materialistic one.

The ceremony took me to the next level. I had never been to one before so I didn't know what to expect. I was nervous, of course, and excited . . . yet I had no expectations. I went in open-minded and with only one thing on my mind, God. When it was over, I was calm, relaxed, with a serene joy that was new to me; and with one thing on my mind, God.

Rudy gave me that "all knowing" smile of his . . . I think, although I did not tell him, that he knew exactly what I was feeling. As time went on, and my trip to South Dakota had ended, and I was in the comforts of my own home again, I could not get all that happened there out of my head; and I didn't want to. I kept adding to my notes, and at night I would sit alone in the dark and just "think." I had come to understand that all the prayers and all the giving of thanks were not only done during times of ceremonies; this is how these people live their lives day in and day out. Each day they are celebrating, giving thanks for the past, present and future . . . and all done humbly and sincerely. It is their belief one should never take anything or anyone for granted. They give thanks in everything, and do all they can to help their brothers, sisters, elders, and, of course, the children along the way.

I would play back step-by-step things that happened, things that were said, things that were done. The fact that I feel so much better now than I did before I went there, and that my medication is cut at least half now from what it was prior to the trip gives, validity to my experience. This became a routine for me, sitting in the dark each night to relax and freeing my mind of all that life can throw us each day. Then I would light my sage, pray . . . and repeat the relaxation and meditation again. Not having children to take care of, I have this luxury.

Every time I do this, or almost every time, thoughts enter my head that make me sit straight up and want to slap myself. I wasn't just praying, I was getting answers. Then it hit me (another slap), God had been talking to me all along! I just didn't know how to listen. The realization of this for me was awesome. It only made me pray more. So much so I asked Rudy, "Think God ever wants me to just shut up?" Now, although I sent this question via email, I know Rudy laughed about it. Of course he wrote me back and said no, to keep praying. Being totally connected to the Creator is how we are suppose to be. It is what He wants.

Rudy has talked about those who are "chosen" ones. Chosen by the Creator to do His will, live by his words and share His love. Rudy is one of the "chosen ones" – as were his mentors. Here is a quote from one of them:

> *I am here by the will of the Great Spirit, and by His will I am chief.*
> *Sitting Bull*

Arvol LookingHorse (another chosen one) was right when he told Rudy this would be a hard life; in many ways when you live and abide by what Creator says, some want to take it upon themselves to create more problems for you. Unless you have a loving relationship with the Creator, it may be difficult to understand why one chooses to do it. Perhaps many love Him so much they can't contain that love within themselves only; they have a need, a drive inside them to share it with others. I would have to say, and I believe it to be true, there are those that choose Creator . . . and then there are those that Creator chooses, Rudy is the latter.

Since he was a small child he has known there was something inside him that was different from the other kids. The adults in his life, especially his mother, knew this. The dreams were only the beginning, almost as if the Creator was preparing him even then for what he would become as a man. Some of the kids teased him over his last name. As he grew up, adults did the same. We humans can certainly treat each other ugly at times. Their words were hurtful when they would say, "You're not even Lakota, your a Mexican." They were half right: Rudy's dad is Mexican, and his mom is Lakota. But in Rudy's mind, and according to the teachings of the One True God, he was one hundred percent God's child, and that was the most important thing to him. He has always chosen his Lakota teachings over any other except for God's. Rudy always put the Creator God first.

> *"You are my witnesses," says the Lord, "And My servant whom I have chosen, That you may know and believe Me,*

> *And understand that I am He. Before Me there was no God formed, Nor shall there be after Me."*
>
> *Isaiah 43:10*

The Bible states in Isaiah 58:1

> *Cry aloud, spare not, lift up thy voice like a trumpet, and shew my people their transgression, and the house of Jacob their sins.*

I asked Rudy, "What about those who don't believe in Christ, but rather hold on to the anger and hate?" His reply was, "Even though one doesn't believe in Him, at least believe in what He did for all of mankind . . . it is a perfect teaching of love and the willingness to take on himself what was meant to be for them. That alone should have them falling in love with Him and His purpose."

While patience is an issue for many of us, it doesn't appear to be for Rudy, not when he is teaching others. I remember the day I had talked to Shrek and asked him, "How did Rudy come to choose the Christian path?" Shrek replied, "He didn't, it chose him, and it chose him many years ago." The seed was planted in him before he was ever born, and the Creator watered it as he grew up. One way of doing so was through his dreams. I think Rudy knew all this even as a small boy; although he didn't understand it, he pretty much grew into it. Understanding began to come when he went to stay with his uncle all those years ago. It's hard for a true Christian to wrap their head around the idea that there are some people that are "offended" by the word of the Creator or even the mention of His name.

Others claim to not believe in Him at all, which doesn't "offend" me, but rather it saddens me. They are tossing away the hope that we as humans cling to, such a belief as there is "more to this life" than just living on planet Earth, dying, and being buried. I'll never believe something in the universe had a bad case of gas and belched loudly to produce the earth and all it contains. What "offends" me are those full of "self-righteous" and want to put an end to or even control the way others are allowed to worship the Creator. These groups removed God from every entity known to us from the government down to the schools. Yet, every time something goes wrong in the world, they are the first to ask, "Where was God when this happened or that happened?" He was on the sidelines watching . . . where mankind has put Him.

Those that are quick to claim that God doesn't exist are just as quick to blame Him for all that goes wrong in the world . . . well, which is it? Does He exist or not? Or has mankind come to use Him as a "catch-all" for all that goes wrong in the world, or perhaps just those times they don't get their way?"

> *Ask, and it will be given to you; seek, and you will find; knock, and it will be opened to you. For everyone who ask receives, and he who seeks finds, and to him who knocks it will be opened.*
>
> *Matthew 7:7–8*

If you want God to protect you, He will. What are you willing to do for Him? Some have the impression the Bible is a book of "don'ts" . . . Don't do this, don't do that, no you can't have this, don't desire that. All I can say is: they have not read it. Rather, they have listened to others that probably haven't read it either. Isn't it time to read the book? Get the answers you are seeking. We must ask in order to receive; they must seek if they wish to find. Perhaps we can "find God" (although He is not lost or missing) on our own, and maybe we don't need someone like Rudy. But my journey would not be the same if I had not met Rudy.

I knew the Creator before Rudy came into my life, but not in the same way. Sure, I knew He existed, and I knew He loved me; I never doubted that. What I doubted was me. Rudy helped me get clarity on this and much more. And now, I not only speak to God, but He speaks back; and because of what I have learned . . . I now "hear Him." Not in a big booming voice that rattles the windows, but with a gentle kindness, a loving way as a Father speaks to a small child. He talks to me in the same voice and southern twang I have. Go figure right? He speaks all languages. How else would He speak to His millions of children if He could not?

This is what Rudy had to say about doubting yourself, I hope it is helpful to you.

> *Never doubt yourself. The Creator created you so you have his power living deep within your flesh and bones,*

to the very core of your spirit. So when others say it can't be done or you can't do it, just remember you can, because the Creator God creates conquerors only – that's why He created you in His image. So like my little son that runs around my home who looks like me, has some of my traits, smile, values and virtues; understand what I'm telling you and it is deep explanation.

We are all little gods from the One True God; little spirits from the Great Spirit. So we have His power and so many real spiritual people have been trying to tell us this for years, and that alone is the connection we have with our Father, our Creator and Thwe Wakan Sica.

The source of all bad doesn't want us to know "this is truth" – don't be afraid of your power. To be who you were created to be – natural born conquerors. Yes, my brothers and my sisters, you are a conqueror; but we must conquer ourselves before we can conquer our goals and our world. Use your power! Walk in a sacred manner and love to the very end – and remember, God the Creator loves you, and so do I.

Itancan Wocekiye Gluha Mani
Chief Walks With Prayers

I got the opportunity to talk to Shrek again. He patiently tolerated and answered my questions.

Q: Where you ever afraid of any of the processes you experienced in becoming a medicine man?
A: Afraid from the get go. It isn't something I ever asked for or wanted. I didn't want the hardships or responsibility. But I was afraid of the consequences if I said no, so I accepted it. I do it out of love for my people, and that is what gets me through it; and the love for my family. Being away from family is hard.
Q: In your opinion, what is the greatest challenge any medicine man faces?
A: Myself, I am my worst enemy, constantly fighting with my spiritual side and human side. The man side of me wants time for me, but I must think like Spirit, not like man.

Q: Is it correct that a medicine man or holy man cannot work a nine-to-five job? Could you explain why this is so?

A: They can, but aren't supposed to. We are to be available to the people at all times. If your boss understands, knows the ways of your job to Spirit . . . it can be done. Spirit comes before the job, before myself, before anything.

Q: Can you share one experience that proved to you that the Creator has a sense of humor?

A: Last year when I got home, a lot of negativity going around, and my truck broke down. I had prayed to get home, and I did . . . by tow-truck. [chuckle]

Q: Has Spirit ever told you no, that you could not help someone?

A: No. They have told me I could not do a ceremony, because it was not needed.

Q: Do all medicine men work together as you and Rudy have done?

A: No they do not . . . but we all should. There is some jealousy there, not between Rudy and I, but others. All want their own way, a power trip of sorts. It shouldn't be that way; we should be working together, and together helping the people. Everyone wants "credit" for the good things done, and that isn't what it's about.

Q: I know you are aware of some of the problems Rudy had in the beginning, some of the name calling, when others said "you're not Lakota, you're Mexican" – can you tell me how this affected those of you who are so close to him, watching him go through this?

A: It is sad to see someone you love go through this kind of thing. Everyone has their teachings. There are those that say it's in the blood line – there is more to it than that. It will follow blood, but it's also genealogy . . . so it may skip a generation or two. Creator chooses the ones He wants, it is not always in the bloodline. All of those starting out go through their trials. It is not an easy path.

Q: I asked Rudy's daughter this question: "There are many who can not come to South Dakota where Rudy is, and don't have the personal connection to him. What can they do in their own life to honor Spirit and mature in their spirituality?"

A: All have the connection; all they have to do is pray. It only takes a few minutes. One doesn't have to be have a holy man, or medicine man, or even Baptist preacher; the one they have to have is God, and He is always there. God has many names given Him by man, we all pray; we call him Creator or Grandfather.

Q: To those who are still fighting God, have not committed to Him, what advice to them could you offer?

A: Believing in the Creator, that is up to the person. It can't be forced. If you don't believe, you will get nothing from Him. Nothing. People expect instant results . . . for those that truly believe, it will come; it will come in the Creator's time, not theirs.

Q: How do you feel about those who put a price tag on ceremonies, sweats, and other things sacred to the Lakota people?

A: I strongly disagree with it. Prayer is a gift from Creator and you can't put a price on that. I don't have the power to give away what was given to me. The items I use in ceremony, those things are not mine, but Creators. I carry these things for the people, to pray for them, and it is the Creator that gave me these things. The bundle belongs to the people . . . I carry it for them, I am just the keeper. It is my responsibility to take care of it.

Shrek's beliefs are strong, as is his conviction, and his dedication to the Creator. You will find this to be the case more often than not, no matter who the man is who has accepted this responsibility – and it is a huge responsibility. When the people come to you for help, you can't say, "Oh, I'm busy right now, come back tomorrow." That isn't how it works. Your life pretty much stops, and its your job to help the one in need.

This can sometimes weigh on the medicine man or holy man, and not just him, but his family as well. It takes a strong woman to be married to, or partnered to, one of these men. They go into it knowing from the start they will never be number one in this man's life, more like third, or even fourth. Rudy's wife, Reba . . . we didn't get to talk as much as we needed to. She was always busy with children, cooking, and doing what Rudy needed her too. At the time she was blessed with her niece being there, who all called "Bubbles." Bubbles was, indeed, adorable, and older than her years. She could do and did do all the things Reba did. I did get to talk to Reba a little bit while I was there and a time or two since then. Here are some questions I asked her.

Q: When did you and Rudy meet, and how?

A: Okay, we met in Rapid City September of '03. He asked me out. I was in a bad relationship before.

Q: How long before you knew he was the man for you, and what made you decide that?

A: I grew up the Christian way and was taught by my mom any other way was bad. It took me awhile to get used to his way, but I learned that it's all the same

Q: Is your spiritual belief the same as Rudy's? And if not, how have you handled this and still have maintain such a good relationship? Not many could do this.

A: It was a blessing 'cause I was alone and didn't know too many things, being only twenty years old with one child and one on the way. I was scared so I believe God brought him to me.

As with any married couple, Rudy and Reba have had their ups and downs. I cannot imagine the stress involved for either of them. Rudy is married to the Creator first, the people second. It is not until somewhere after this his own wife and children come into the picture. Not a lot of couples today could survive this. If you are a firm believer in the Bible though, you will see that many men lived this way. Some never married at all; this is how powerful the love of the Creator they had, always putting God first and not thinking of themselves, but rather what God wanted for them, and following the instructions of living that the Creator provided for them.

One of the highlights of the trip for me at the time, and even since I've been home, has been Rudy's mother, Mrs. Janis. She is just "Mom" to me now. A true blessing in my life she has been, and I got to talk to her the other day. She was at Rudy's house and she was cooking for everyone there, and there was a full house as Rudy prepared for a ceremony later that evening. She made time for me, as busy as she was, and even answered a couple of questions for me.

Q: If your young grandson were to come to you and say he was going to be a medicine man or holy man, what advice would offer him?

A: I'd tell him the truth. It is a hard road to walk, and they would have to be willing to give up a lot of things. But . . . if they have the calling, it is what they should do.

Q: What, to you . . . is the most important experience that could happen to or for Rudy in his life time?

A: I believe it is what he is doing now. The spirits are coming to him – God's helpers – and he needs to listen to them; and I think he does.

Q: I remember you telling me Rudy's grandparents were very spiritual, and his paternal grandmother was a "holy woman." What can you tell me about them and the influence they had on Rudy's life?

A: One of them was his great-grandmother in Mexico. She was a huge influence on him, a positive one, although I don't think he realized it at the time – but I'm sure he does now.

Tonight I got a wonderful surprise; I was able to talk to Rudy's sister, Sabrina. She impressed me, and I would have to say she is a combination of both Rudy and their mom. Her voice has that familiar smoothness to it and she was sincere in her responses. I look forward to speaking with her again.

Q: Do you remember any of the abuse Rudy went through as kid? Or hearing about it?

A: We were all treated badly by our stepmother, and we stayed with my uncle a lot, and on weekends would go to Dad's. She wanted her kids to be noticed and we were shoved in the darkness, as to not be seen or noticed.

Q: Do you recall his wild days as young man when he was living out the gangsta life? Share what you can with the reader.

A: I remember some of it, but not everything.

Q: How old were you when Rudy went to jail, and what do remember about it?

A: Don't remember my age at the time. When he went to jail, he had time to think. I remember them locking him up and transferring him; they put him on a helicopter and transferred him to another jail out of state.

Q: Once he was out of jail, and his way of thinking and his way of living had changed, what impact did this have on you and your life, if any?

A: I had my own problems trying to raise kids, trying to help my mom. She had my youngest son, so we were all trying to get by the best we could.

Q: Your mom has told me all her children are Christians, but Rudy also walks the Red Road. Has his choice had any influence on you or your spirituality?

A: My grandmother was a pipe holder, my grandfather was a medicine man. She had left on her own, and all that was found was her clothes and bones.

One day I woke up, tired of living the way I had been. A woman would come by with a Bible, and we would read and talk, I believe in both ways. In the end, it's all the same.

Q: How does it make you feel when/if you see others questioning his "Indianness" for lack of a better word, because he is a Christian?

A: They don't know us, they are the type that enjoy dragging others down. We are half Mexican, and we are half Lakota, and we are Christian.

Q: Could you describe your brother and the importance of what he is doing? Tell me from a sister's point of view the impact you think he has had on the people. Not only the Lakota people, but all people since all races and all walks of life are listening to him and learning from him . . .

A: I know he is doing good, I like what he's doing, and he is good at it.

Q: What was one of the most valuable lessons your mother taught all you growing up as a child?

A: To respect others and treat them the way we want to be treated, especially the elders.

Q: Have you been a witness to one of the miraculous healings Creator gave another using your brother as the vessel?

A: Yes, I had what the doctor called Bell's Palsy. Rudy gave me a treatment for it and its been gone since then.

Q: What was the one occasion in your opinion that your mother felt the most proud of Rudy?

A: When he found his way, leaving the bad behind. He didn't give up. To this day he is still going through it, even with those that challenge him or are jealous of him.

Q: Tell me in your opinion about the times Rudy was leading the gangsta life, what was your biggest fear for him?

A: Him getting hurt or worse, and, of course not knowing where he was at most of the time.

I talked to a married couple that was there at the Sundance, Rose and Bryan Butler. I asked them several questions also and found their answers inspiring. I'll share that interview with you now. Rose was a huge factor in my being at the Sundance this past summer; she was one-third of the "Team God" that conspired to get me there. Yes, it's true: Rose, Rudy, and the Creator Himself make a fine team.

Q: Rose, how did the two of you come to know Rudy?

A: On the Internet I saw a post he made and sent him a friend request.

Q: Can you tell me what impressed you about him, to the point of you wanting to get to know him better?

A: The words he was saying in regards to God rang true; know that, and his demeanor. He didn't just talk, he walked the talk. He lived it and breathed it; everything he did revolved around God.

Q: How and when did you learn of his being a Holy man?

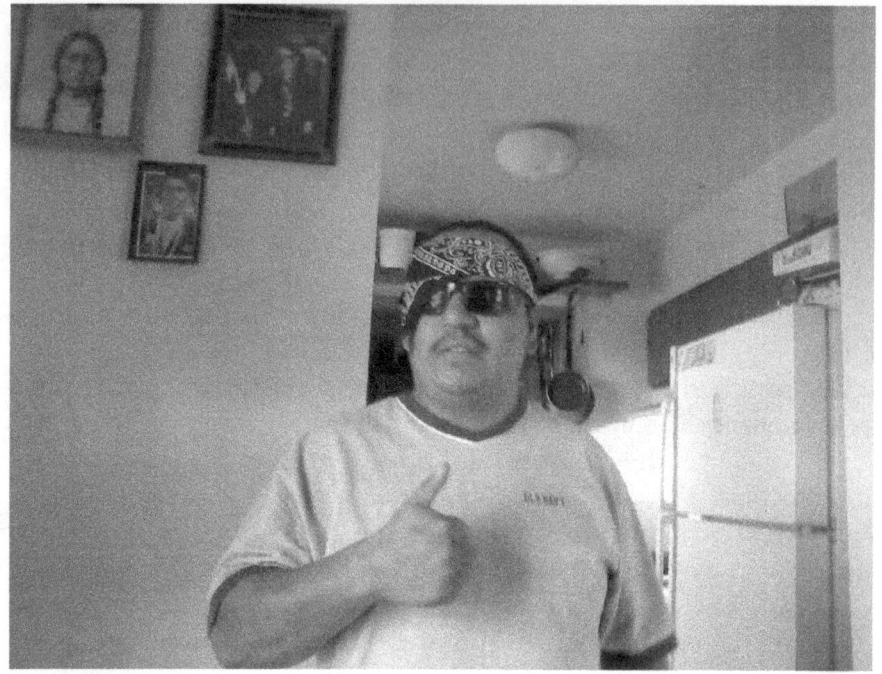

A: Didn't know at first. He was talking about the prophecies . . . I just watched him after that to see if he was another guru medicine man. Rudy told me to call him, and he talked a while, and I knew by talking to him he had some answers I had been looking for. He used scripture to explain things to me.

Q: Did you believe it right away? Or were you suspicious since some claim to be what they are not?

A: I just didn't know at first, that is why I watched him for awhile. He follows the old way, the authentic old way of the Lakota . . . he followed the way Spirit instructed him, and the way I wanted to learn and to follow. He was very patient in his teachings, very open, not holding back.

Q: Which of you got to know him first, Rose or Bryan?

A: Rose.

Q: What was the one convincing factor for each of you that Rudy was the real deal?

A: When he came to my house, to do a ceremony and asked nothing in return.

Q: Since not all medicine men or even holy men are Christian, what did you think when you realized Rudy is indeed a Christian?

A: At first I thought it was odd, then I thought "why not?" Then I realize in ceremony, it was very similar to the crucifixion. Before the ceremony, when he was talking and explaining things to us, he read scripture during this time, and then he took the time to explain it to us. He said the prophets in the Bible had visions, and how Moses went up on the mountain to talk to God. It gave us understanding of what our path is about.

Q: When you see others challenge him on his beliefs . . . what is your opinion of how this "holy man" handles these types of situations?

A: He never raises his tone; he is humble, grateful and dignified.

Q: When did you first meet him in person and how, if at all, did your opinion of him change or improve?

Q: Met him first when he came to our house to do a ceremony. When he did come here, I was worried what he thought of us, but he was just a regular guy. His love of children became obvious by the way he treated our kids. When he woke up in the morning, he didn't have to put his "spiritual face" on, and he didn't pray like many at certain times, he prayed All The Time. The way Bryan took to him, and learned from him was surprising. We have seen fakes before, and this was not the case with Rudy. There is nothing fake about him.

Q: Knowing you have heard at least some, if not all, of Rudy's story (some call it a testimony), if one of your sons or grandsons wanted to follow in Rudy's footsteps, how would feel about this?

A: Very comfortable. My daughters are following this path.

Q: Bryan, in your opinion, how does one "become a holy man" or medicine man?

A: You are one if God gives you this gift, you can't buy it, or practice it to perfection, and it isn't handed down through generations. Either God anoints you to be one, or He doesn't.

Q: What is the most valuable lesson both of you have learned from/through Rudy, and would you share that with the readers please?

A: We are all related and we should all watch out for and help each other. And the spirituality, once you jump in . . . it is something that is not to be taken lightly. Once you commit yourself to that, then you are committed, and there is no turning back. You have to hold the pipe with both hands, you can't just hold it with it one.

A year has gone by . . .

After a bumpy plane ride to South Dakota, I was glad to see my friends and family at the airport to meet me. A year has gone by since I saw them last, and it was as refreshing as a cold drink of water on hot day to see them now. They hadn't changed a bit, Rudy was his usual easy going self, his wife Reba was also the same, on a mission; and Rose, well . . . seeing Rose is sort of like finding your favorite shirt again after its been missing for too long. You're elated to have it back and can't wait to wear it again. We got my luggage and scurried off to Wal-Mart to pick up a few things.

Being back at the house, and in my spot in the camper with Bryan, Rose, and the kids was like returning home once more. It was a warm feeling in my soul. The place was busy, inside and outside. People coming and going, talking and laughing, deep conversations and the kids darting between adults, each one on an adventure all their own. It took all I had to not cry when I saw Mom again – Mrs. Janis, Rudy's mother. We had talked a few times in the past year on the phone, but it was time for me to collect my hug. I had waited a year for that hug . . . and it felt great.

Another Mending The Sacred Hoop was underway and Sundance would start in a couple of days. That meant there was a lot of work to be done, and once it started . . . twice the work to be done. There were thirteen dancers this year, each making their own sacrifice, and each with their own story to tell. Gaining understanding within themselves . . . and of the Creator God. New friends were made, new family members met, and more prayers sent up than of all of us could have counted. Better yet, those prayers were heard and answered.

The dancers stepped to the drum beat for four long days, and on the last day Mom adopted me into her family. What an honor and beautiful experience that was. My tears could not be held back that day, and I tear up just thinking about it. Mom gave me her Lakota name and she made me the most gorgeous star quilt I've every laid my eyes on; along with some jewelry she made me that matched it. She wrote me a letter that I will cherish 'til my dying day and which is now in a frame. This adoption not only is an honor, but comes with responsibility. I now have many brothers and sisters, nieces and nephews, and a mom I did not have before; and as with any family, when they need you . . . its your responsibility to be there for them.

Rudy taught all of us while I was there, and he teaches with a great amount of patience. I noticed the more he teaches, the more enthralled he becomes. He lights a room up with his passion for the Creator and for his family. There really is nothing more important to him. He is a loyal and dedicated man. "Be careful with your words," he said. "Be careful what you think, you become what you think," he continued. He would slow down and sound out certain words for us to learn and then tell us the appropriate time to use them. In all his time he spent with each us there during this very sacred time he was no stick-in-the-mud. There were times I laughed 'til my belly hurt, and at other times I listened with fascination as he spoke to all there. No one had to wonder what to do, what was expected of them, or where they would be . . . he explained to each person as it was needed.

I know Rudy received phone calls once the Sundance had come to an end complimenting him on how he handled himself . . . and the "old school" way he runs the Sundance and all the ceremonies. He isn't one to take credit for much of anything really, and his basic reply to these kind of statements is a short one, "That's my job . . . ." He gives all the praise to the Creator God and says he is simply doing what he is led to do.

So many are hungry for "something" and many aren't sure what that "something" is . . . until they feel it for the first time. It's one thing to claim to believe; its another to walk and talk with the Creator and feel Him with you . . . and know He is talking back to you. The first time you pay attention to that little voice and you do what it says and the fountain of love and blessings is opened to you, it will be a moment in time you will never forget.

This year was busier than last year. There were more people so there was more work. This meant more cooking to be done, more kids playing, and more blessings to be received. Shrek couldn't make it this year. I missed him, as did the others. There were more tents set up on the Sundance grounds, more dancers – thirteen this year – and many more prayers were sent up.

Mom danced on the last day, and this too was the day of my adoption ceremony and Joseph's. Rudy adopted him, and my heart was full of love for them both as I stood behind them and watched. Joseph now has his own little son, another new addition to an already big family; and he once again sang and drummed the entire four days as did Jonathan and Rudy's next to youngest son, Lonnie.

How I love my Lakota family and the blessings the Creator has bestowed on me that are too many to count or share. The loyalty I feel for them I'm not sure I can put into words. The magnitude of love that exist in this family is not something one can really put into words; however, all feel it when they come around.

Even the high winds that rocked the camper to and fro were not enough to prevent any there from the prayer, ceremony, dancing, singing, and laughter of good times and beautiful memories being made. The faces I can still see, the drums I can still hear, the sage and cedar I can still smell, and the hugs I can still feel.

Not one there has not had hard times in this life and yet they hold no resentment or bitterness for it. All have been broken by heartache and yet they still love; all have been sick and yet healed, and all have been lost and now found. It is true what they say . . . "A family that prays together, stays together."

The pain and heartache this family has gone through did not make all of us the loving family we are today. The Creator God did. It isn't tradition or religion that have gotten us all through the poverty, bad relationships, and the beatings life has handed us at times . . . but it was the Creator God that has gotten us through it all. And it isn't relatives or mentors or inheritance that has made Rudy the dedicated, loyal, servant of his people, and his family . . . it was the Creator God.

If you long to have the love, the family, and the countless blessings spoken of here, . . . there is only one way; and that is to pray. Pray to the one true Creator of all things, the God of love, the God of all . . . and Ask. Remember, one must do their part . . . Living your life for the Creator God, putting Him first in all you do, and following His word may not be the easiest thing to do, but it is more than worth it. As Mom said, "Know your place . . . you are not better than or stronger than the Creator . . ."

Being in hell on earth is not where you want to be. This "hell on earth" was not just a place that Rudy visited for a time, but he lived there for many years. The "valley of the shadow of death" was his home. The gansta life style was the only life as an adult that he knew, and his childhood was equal to that of war zone in a third world country – never knowing from day to day as a child or an adult if it would be his last day on earth or not. It was at his lowest point, in the darkness and in a lonely jail cell that the hand of God reached out to him, touching his very soul and scooping him up into His nail-scarred hands, and offered him not only a better life, but eternal life.

The Creator God can and will do the same for you. He has no limitations . . . and living "in the shadow of the valley of death" is not His plan or desire for you. Rudy had the will, the hunger, and just enough strength to say yes and take his power back . . . . will you?

> *Therefore lay aside all filthiness and overflow of wickedness, and receive with meekness the implanted word, which is able to save your souls . . .*
>
> *James 1:21*

www.ingramcontent.com/pod-product-compliance
Lightning Source LLC
Chambersburg PA
CBHW031433040426
42444CB00006B/794